Vocalises

 UpSet Press, Inc.
P.O. Box 200340
Brooklyn, NY 11220
www.upsetpress.org

Copyright © 2012 by Jenny Husk
All poems written by Jenny Husk
Cover artwork by Erin Carney (www.erincarney.net)
Cover and text design by Aaron Kenedi

UpSet Press is an open and supportive space for artists who offer new visions in written language. The press produces mainly first books and newly revised editions of exceptional out-of-print books. Founded in 2000 by a group of NYC-based poets, the press conducts regular poetry workshops and group readings around the city.

Library of Congress Control Number: 2011936803

First printing, 2012
ISBN 978-0-9760142-4-9
Printed in the USA
10 9 8 7 6 5 4 3 2 1

for Nik

CONTENTS

TWO: SEVEN HEADACHES

THREE

FOUR

FOREWORD

How write from inside the heart of crises? Particularly when the heart of crises is both the heat of the body and the hell of the mind? Jenny Husk's poetry reminds us, in spite of all of our attempts to convince ourselves otherwise, that crises is really the only place from which to write, from which to read, from which to think, from which to be. "If you aren't scared sixty percent of the time/you're not alive" a speaker in one of the poems in Joseph Donahue's *Before Creation* opines, to which Jenny Husk responds "Bear in mind all journeys/are perilous." Because of her book I'm bearing that in mind now. Getting from the apartment to the store, the night to the morning, the diagnosis to the cure, one coast to the other coast, be it in an aged plane that may be the vector of complicated socio-political forces or back on the ground, paralyzed between the scarred earth and the human domes, in a car that only appears to be moving ... what carefulness all this requires. Husk's poetry is rich in care for each word it offers and is honest enough to offer up no guarantees that the journey is going to be completed.

Certainly the journey between selves is fraught with risk. "The space between us   is tectonic" she writes. Her poems pay close attention to the wall of sensations that is both pleasure and pain, a wall that isolates us inside experience, since experience is always inside the self as opposed to between two or more individuals. In that sense the tectonic shifts under the house or the highway or the head release us from such prisons, even as they destroy established relationships and anything else we might take for granted. Husk's poems try to help us remember that everything is in constant flux and that these tectonic shifts are both destructive and liberating. "Tears stratify/conversation (steep echoes linger in the fall)," she writes. How speak with one another in the midst of crises? How quiet the trembling body when words are required of us, not simply trepidation and worry? There is no more pressing question.

How live inside the heart of crises? In "Blood Orange" Husk writes:

> Plant an orange tree
> in the black hole
> that belongs to us…

I have to think she means it when she insists on both "the blood" and "the orange," the "planting" and the "hole," one's individual and our common lot, seed and ceasing-to-be. "I love and I hate," as in Catallus, but this is also more than the paradox of desire. It is the paradox of health: to be ill and to be alive in one and the same instant, where to be alive must mean that something is going right. The heaviness of the body is a constant presence here, a presence that the poetry works to undermine through its own tectonic, but never seeks to dissolve or ignore. Such that:

> Fever is fascinating,
> an internal warrior
> against whatever twists
> the body…

Because of my desire to want the body to be whole, because of my need to imagine a being evolving towards its proper form, due to my poetic enthusiasm for transformation and change, thanks to a capacity for making passage to the other, I see these poems as important way stations on the perilous journey they chart. At the same time, as Guido

Ceronetti writes, "Optimism is like carbon monoxide, suffocating us, leaving rose marks around the throat," a flaw in the theology of optimism and hope that Husk's poem also always remind us of. When breath itself is not taken for granted, as happens in these poems, each moment writhes and twists, dancing in the pit of sickness and expectation. "Only this dark warm cave,/ built upon coals in the common bed,/ can carry you into the next weakness." The raid on the inarticulate has never seemed so necessary.

– Leonard Schwartz

ONE

Rescue of Birds and Identity

A current

certain pegged branches   of the mind   uplifted rails,

swatched color—like choice.

A mutant commute   comes
crashing,

ice-flooded

a voice box

tracks distant stares, becomes yesterday   lips slide and push—

cart the noise   belled into glares   a vibration

met at the tip   of a scream.

INHABITING

Bear in mind all journeys
are perilous. I didn't really
know where I was when I emerged
from the woods, but something
told me to keep walking,
tiptoeing through violins.
Eventually, you see, I would
fear, somewhere far off, a pool
of silence in which I'd drown,
after calculating its reach.
Not a death so much as a
terror at sounding alone.
Underneath the panic I might
wonder if my hands would do,
if the fingers were stretchable,
dip-able. Could they shovel out
the mystery? Then, of course,
interrupted, the climax would be
drooled upon by rain, although
necessary, ending the all-so-survivable
peril. But, in which case,
the journey no longer having a mind
to bear, ceased.

RED

Lips canonized to tell an epic lie—to get lost at the root
of all things, fall tear-streaked and naked
in the trash with raw meat, blood tokens of our nature, and a map
to the forest of instinctual addiction—
iron gate/female tongues.

Give us a sign—a stop sign to redden our brakes,
bruise our cheeks (a table to eat at, out of). Hunger
makes us vampires in the tar
as our necks become bound
to hold us up.

There is nothing left
of our skin, our fiber gone (each other emptied).
Vitamin deficient and dressed in swollen scars
of shoes on faces, faces on floors, doors to cross
our eyes with.

There is only one scene in many trips
to the bathroom where blood-stained panties
have lived a thousand times in cells of dying
cells, deposited onto one another. We're suffocating
in cotton.

Woman Looking in the Mirror

Still and staring

(beautiful images fit
comfortably, lounge long,
bathe in its one large eye)

while it reflects myriad symmetries.
Implores: enjoy.

No longer oil on canvas, but blood
on body. Take out, cover up. Put in,
cover up.

Beauty drawn blue deep, bone deep,
blood deep—transfashioned
into a mercurial reflection:
vapid, dim, and strange.

It's the ultimate masterpiece,
an innocent duckling cut in the gut.
The beauty of wounds.

Mirror: now water,
now fillable with a face.

UNTITLED

Your mother licked the sidewalk after I emptied heroin there
from a dirty needle. I should've stitched her curiosity
to the neighbor's cat, I hate that cat. Then, I wouldn't have to hear
your mother's voice tell stories like Cliff's Notes,
like blackberry stains in a fiberglass bathtub, which you keep
washing with, from that same sidewalk, a stone.

VOICE

Stretch through the music,
fall deep in the body where sound
can be touched—inside (the very bottom
a new space). Laid out sharp
and shiny, a reflection vast
as atmosphere—opening up the other side
of silence. Breath takes in the task—a yawn
phrasing flat roads slick
as distance.

THE SPACE BETWEEN

The space between us   is tectonic
changing like the ocean's level
but not at all as dangerous
no faults to fall
into   no wandering
around the emptiness   at the edges
the underground movement   flutters of recollection
time not wasted on measuring   memory
but moments projecting
their figures frail and constant

we are connected   one on this side

one hanging on at the water

separate   but touching inconsistently
desperate whistles   tornadoic dance
running towards the ground and back up
where space is breaking in two   a new void
fighting to fill itself with growth
and green as it is   we're afraid of getting lost
the unknown secret of   remaining seeped
fear of   evaporation

Van Gogh Knows

An instrument is like antacid
for the soul, and
I'm alive because my voice has been stitched
to a sack of karma
filled with haziness and smoke.

But, I do not choke on the menthol
or see the wintergreen mist,
which my lung would like to piss on.
Listen, I want to say, I do not choke.

The freak is normal in noise, where
bald melodies grow brash
at 4:08 a.m., and lay snug in a pore
on the staff FACE.

So, push time between my teeth
to save "Time in a Bottle" of bones,
crunching chord and chord, living
life "Straight outta Compton."

A song can live like that and
smell like fresh freight train graffiti
because music is a halo, torn and perfect,
more intimate than masturbating.

Try plunging into the sound hole of a guitar
and you'll come out whole,
whole enough to hear drums are symbols,
cymbals of man on man—war.

Listen for rooms of dust being picked atom by atom,
harmony. Imagine that,
hack the map, arrangement scream:
geographical, astronomical,
tag it city-wide.

I want to say, I do not choke
as Vincent Van Gogh's "The Starry Night"
eddies a sky-song, song, song.

WORDS

Unlabeled, tied tight, and stacked,
a trash heap of tired flesh
eating and becoming and hating itself.

I take a flashlight
up to this attic and move it around
like a mooneye trembling in its socket.

How dark it gets in here,
air a thick dragline silk.
Endless windows

tar-pasted, black with grease.
And pocketed patches
of darkness conspire

to consume the entire space.
I use the time to taste
the viscous maze I built, lick

the brush down like a cat's guilty tongue
on fur, cleaning and tasting and touching itself.
Cobwebs support the emptiness,

fill it in at the corners, lock
down its lexis.
And I, a brown recluse,

am at home, free in the dust
of my mesh.
The shadows line up
to clean my mouth of its hunger,
but I wonder about its appetite
to give, eat something more than—words.

LIES TRAPPED IN A PENCIL SHARPENER

Folding thoughts into frogs
easy as paper
on a Dexatrim high
who will you kiss—slick as seal skin
you, who win all tongue twisters
in origami tent-making

Vocalises

WOMAN STANDING IN THE UNEMPLOYMENT LINE

I understand my rights, I get it.
I'm as guilty this year as I was in 1902,
existing in a hallowed-out cherry pit,
stapled, juiced and my mouth bled through.

Said Yes ten years ago, now I'm a tour,
a mansion to be traipsed about and slogged.
Married to marriage, but no diamonds to abhor.
The wedding began and ended; I was mugged.

Now I stand in this line, no milk for my kids
and I wait for my number to be called out;
empty voices, from the breast, scrawling bids
like colors falling from a mountain of drought.

DEATH UNTIL

Rich virulent maid
strewn without concern,
fell off the rack the week she coughed up
sacred pictures.

He, master of memory,
sunned out a door,
as though he had gone in a dream
one-hundred steps below
his starting point;
she found the wreckage,

scared, not scared
to die together after forty,

overflowing, closed, distant,
they traveled on extravagant dirt.
Two off to stampede water
from the toes of the deliverer.

Vocalises

Until Death

From the toes of the deliverer;
two off to stampede water.
They traveled on extravagant dirt,
overflowing, closed, distant,

to die together after forty,
scared, not scared.
She found the wreckage,
his starting point;
one-hundred steps below
as though he had gone in a dream,

sunned out a door,
he, master of memory,

Sacred pictures
fell off the rack the week she coughed up.
Strewn without concern,
rich virulent maid.

THAT PIECE OF SKIN

Border built of raw tissue
perfecting the flesh-hold.
Flesh tightened to fight you
like a fist closing in
on an argument.
Chastity—a bandaged canal:
thick as blackness.

I just want it back
to see if I need it,
if I could use it against
you against my body.

But I only see you,
flesh standing in flesh.
My piece of skin ruptured
to open the room bloodied
for your passage,
your skin muscled
for the wet trip.

Mine was soft as a peach once,
before you poured
the first white mixture
of milky cement,
sweat and spit too. This
to make it more your own,
to take it home with you.

Give it back to me.
That mark of my birth, scarred.

DARK ROOM

You look at the T.V. static, I see you stop breathing.
Smell of electricity you cannot see.
Torture-couch under my back, you say, prickly.

Sit up, shadow, and tell
me about all the hands you've seen! Where is the catalogue?
Have you misplaced your favorite box?

Now, I see you've stopped breathing out
is all. I could recommend someone, if you'd like. A doctor
for red face and oxygen overdose. I am good at that, too,
recommendations I mean. Now, where are your hands,
and what have they touched
since last confession?

Velvet shoes and cold barrettes, and nothing else I swear.
Just putting clothes on and taking them off
and putting them on again, you tell me.

I hear the T.V. static.
I see the shades of black and white
move around like your shadow, on the earth, and I cannot breathe.

1979

An orange, orange atmosphere fogs
this 5x7 world.
There are no blinks of white,
just one tinctured tint—antique.
Even our eyeballs could have been dipped
in tea, pressed into our caramel face—chemicalized.
And our hair looks to have been
shaped and heated to set like bronze.

Two golden statues, two smiles,
two children, motionless.

ENJOYING LONELINESS

So the words are not what they could be,
but it's okay because I listen
to Coltrane.
I've no need to speak, then.
Just push my toe to the wood floor
and roll onto my heel
as leverage to loosen a flame
so I can burn up another menthol light,
have another Love Supreme
and build a film of smoke across my eye
like a story to tell myself
while Elvin Jones is tripping the drum
like a cough I'd love to have.
It's so satisfying to climb
off the bail of nicotine with those low strings
so slow and I know the sax
has all the notes I don't in the end.
I listen instead and breathe the beat
and wait
for the Marlboro Man
and his tobacco handkerchief.

BLOOD ORANGE

Plant an orange tree
in the black hole
that belongs to us.
Hope hunger,
breathe fruit
into earth.
Stillness
strumming
underneath.
Trunk roots shade
in dark, there.
White silence streams
the black hole—like water,
swims.
We drown
in its false shoulder,
dangerously soft.
Blood juice,
sliced light—leaves flicker,
fly, fall,
cannot express their color.
And here grows,
how it grows, this bark,
no glow
upon its heat, no fruit,
no blood to swallow.
Just a hole,
a pitch, pitch hole.

TWO: SEVEN HEADACHES

Vocalises

Ear on the edge—delicate glass. Vibrations
of a melting glacier.

Infected (green and flooded)
with dead-ends and plug-ups to dance on.

It smells like steel, a metal factory
where sparks weld my thoughts
into locked doors. Strange

sterling ache—temples crushed
by scales in overload. Think 'til the mind
falls apart. Pieces of rock

and hook blacken in the tumble
through blinding days

and I have few signs.

Temples stretched tight as a drum,
wall-to-wall reverberation,
repetition makes forgetting impossible,
it has a rhythm, it moves—tap, taptap, taptap, taptaptap.
Ricochet-pain on pain, skin beaten to test its tautness,
vibration chisels memory flicker to flake
splintering place and time, keeping its status
at the center of the tactus.

Aging fast as rock
with fewer breaths between the pain,
growing fire and weeping blinks
make an artist out of it.

No gasping wound, no flooding,
no blood. There is a delicate
nature to it, comes on like an adjustment.
The mind slowly aware of its physicality, overheats.

Too much intake or too little?
It wants attention,
nudges, until even breath feels carried.
No bag of feathers.

One-ton eyelids lift and crash, only half-lift, fall into thorny skin.
Been watering the big organ since morning, all silk and sap—this
sticky mess. Sore-throat tension brings in the air and pushes it back
into its completeness, outside. Where's the moon-tug in daylight?
Single pendulum swing carries the weight away. Its return is elastic,
unreal, and still the same motion. One long burden dying in the
open gravity like a wound, if heals, will make you disappear. Can't be
sure to live without this brick in the shoulder, tearing concentration
from its seat, unruly dictator of this constant twitch.

Decibels click, slowly chip into the quiet mess, the unabandonable silence always destroyed—eternally interrupted.

Within the fog, the world seems watery and interlineating. No surface, no third dimension. Try crying, and it's the same.

Time is measured in the head; in the ache that it was, becomes, or forgets to let go of. Pressure taps on the fore and reconfigures its way in, every time.

An eye is a hammer—loses hold of the nails that pour out this side of trauma; an eye that won't stop seeing, stop metering out the scenes, the beat that stays on repeat.

It's a distinct moment when even the thought of light is too bright to hold in the mind, too heavy to drop off into memory.

Forgotten musculatures knot and petrify. Days atrophy and green off at their ends. And lost moments collapse into themselves, clones of one another.

Things often consent to lining up—attracted to balance and its teetering opposition so close to taking over, but the blind spot holds the ache in refuge.

Heavily weighted head, bears down: an iron competition.
Lead leans into temple, cheeks, and eyes like myth.
Compressing all infinite sides
of itself, it wrestles, works its way in—planting
the pain, growing it easily.
Don't know where to tackle it, can't find its feet,
its hands all rock about the skull.

Vocalises

Keeps scooping me out.
Has a way of compacting all the ringing

into one millisecond and there it is
everywhere I turn—entering,

keeps digging deep for silence
when the light chimes in, flows

like a fire alarm, my hydrant rusted
and a drought in my throat

but it keeps me empty
the rest of the week,

going by like a day with no shade.

THREE

AT AND JUST BELOW
after Erin Carney

Tears stratify
conversation (steep echoes linger in the fall).

Rising colors that never sound. Silent clear
water foams under such eruption.

River dialogue. Glare on the surface.

Memory becomes memory. A boat closing in
on its own weight,   flood and floating.

Listening condenses.

A drowning decision—straddled in rain.
(Sighs grow ample enough to say)—

African Sky

Earth flings her teeth
because she cannot speak—voice exiled
to shine in a silent void. Shapes
emboss blackness and move bodies
bold as truth—enshrine history,
weak from screaming, into brilliant white points
of distance kept high, and rarely viewed.
Ignored by day, forgotten. Constantly plowing
space, crying to be heard,
feeling only the crowded violence
of separation from gravity. No comfort
surrounds empty night.

RAIN

The sky greens
and slides heavy as satin—screaming,
laden with effort
to wet the empty avenue, to struggle.
Granite rain stapling
the ground to itself, rock to rock
where the storm pushes
through its own lung, spills electricity
with a subterranean yawn
that paddles across the Hudson—river-lifted
under every cloud's floated weight.
Lightning leans on the atom wall,
fogged into visibility—
and to the sky's hidden light,
infinite reflections keep falling.

Waiting for Ground Break

Quiet skin binds book-rinds
around snake-fruit
where the sun peels before orange April.
Dirt isn't allowing visitors
this hour—space trapped in the garden hose.
Empty house swelled with tiptoes
along the windowsills, twenty rooms
stained in prints: in ache to exit.
Ants lay eggs at the yard's eye,
where soil looks for new seeds.
Breeding begins on the fortieth morning,
juiced in life and pomegranates.

In-Between

The wind cantillates
like a violin—reminisces.
No special words or show of grief,
just brief sobs letting go
as they decorate the sky.

Night, with its shadows
floats around, wrapped
in plical spaces between clouds.

Folded darkness loosens and staggers
into time—lingers in the transition.
Time continually spills the two extremes
(sight and sightlessness) until they are whole,
but separate
and pure—distilled and washed, clean as space.

The white sun
glowing mountainous and cold,
losing its feathers, does not understand
the difference.

ADVERSARIES

She coldly stares down the street lamp as his gaze
flickers on, begins competition for ruler of the unlit time,
but her feminine bulb breaks before the new moon,
and his light staggers with the changing of glass
(watts of hysterical power), making many fires disappear
into florescent lungs that keep Orion searching
for his belt, and the guarded moon, leaning farther
for her reflection, fading in the falsity of a fire-breathing
dragon, light slaying light.

LINGERING

The flash sustains, a pulsing
plants itself behind eyes.
Electric-memory runs and the pupil
clicks on, on and on. The body refuses
to let the present become past; it hangs
lash to lash. The moment lags
on the weight of waiting.
Flanks of time float through canals,
but this internal image won't degrade.
An abstract sky emerges.
Strobes grow green under each blink. Can't rub the light out.
It falls, though—deep in the center of the lens's flash.

FRAGILE

When the first string on my guitar snaps
down cold to release my body heat
onto a white palm,
I am stricken.
I am stricken by the thought: my finger picks
the strings as my brain
picks my fingers—a machine of a machine, and
who is the "I" of my eye?
The cut on my hand lies open
and swollen in the shape of some
unintelligible winged or lipped thing,
bleeding full,
tapering when tired,
just like when my feminine insides decide
to become external
and spit themselves red
onto the porcelain.
My face
steals the color of water stain
and slips in
when too much blood
visits the air. Then I pull close to my center,
relax, let it go.
Reflex. Ugh, ugh, ugh.
Muscles plunge empty
my center
into the porcelain.

PRESERVED

Stains like memory   wear away,
floating seconds   a million shivers.
A tear strikes   and in its pool, could
fluoresce   a new purity of purpose,
bind   another empty page to ink.

LISTEN TO THIS

People are breathing.
There are air-guzzling lungs in the tar center of a city,
liquid heat citied in the mouths of children.

Have you ever heard
of silk striping every resemblance of a worm?
The dress worms its way out of that, right?

I worry about firing the stove,
a vision too hot to touch, unless you're the source,
and gas makes you blow blue,
a fire flower, iron-raked.

Have you ever had to swim
in a mirror with waves cut
from diamonds, diamonds bought as gifts,
guilt rifts?

Do you ever drown
in the bed you make, stop the sheets
from making paper-cuts of your words?

AMERICAN HISTORY

Every side is just one more side
of the story. We only needed six
before we built the box to hide it all away. It's perfect.
Tinseled in trumpets and money,
flags, and "Who are ya's?"
A beautiful package, artistic and unique.
One by one we stepped in—careful
not to be stone—careful not to scratch
the bottom. (It may be fiberglass, or baby oil.
It might be esoteric or alive.)
We went about our business,
map-making and picture-taking.
Spring came and greened our view.
Then, we forget the box
and believe we have, again, discovered
the newest world.

MEMORY

Like stepping into a labyrinth I see you as I would see
your choices, all the turns you must've taken, all the steps
you did not; your caterpillar self unknowingly wraps you up
in the mask for waiting, and then the big debandaging,
the crack in the sap, unsticky, slippery wings
inch the sides, escape into the inevitable, but it's leaving home
and trauma is still there, like a canoe whose oars scratch the waves
that become its own wing.
You circle the shell you must leave behind
and enter a new phase, a magic trick, a true sense of losing
or evolving or manifesting
movement—the only way out.

Woman On Safari

She wanted the perfect picture, and she might have gotten it, but all we have is this story. A woman steps out into the desert to kneel with the sitting lions, to snap their essence into a camera and take it home with her—to feel their simple courage, and their weight spread like territory; their fur floating like grains of sand caught in the current of heat; their claws sinking into earth like a fort of thorns. She walks. Her husband and children waiting, a little anxious and adrenalized, hoping she's done every time they hear the sush-tick of her camera, see the glassy-eyed lions take a long, strong stretch. They seem so tired, so worthless, like the last clinging coals in the fire, asthmatic. She is unafraid, rises, satisfied, only to turn and see their renewed flames flying at her, red and wild, fierce and determined to take her essence with them, claim theirs back from their burned permanence.

FOUR

SEQUINED PULSE

Light burns and ages. Eyes wade through the soot.

Tick tick, a real tilt of the drill.   Easy depth,   bottomless gravity.

      Search

and tunnel to a horizontal summit.

Old posture a reflection (symmetric).   A different kind of

recession—the collapse

      of high-tide.

Pearlized breath, held so long

in the warm buds of fleshy silence,   becomes stolid.

Cracked coral,

buried in time's meridian, incapable of shallow recovery   (the sea),

canyons through slow-witted nights—digs fissures,

builds answers layer under layer   of distance. And opens.

INSOMNIAC NIGHTMARE

Chapped boredom's bedtime
turning and tossing thoughts out
in reprimand to go back and tell the others
"We're closed." Never mind the potent stuff,
archived voices cry by number.

Tossing healed-bone headaches
to open tight-jaw when flecked screams
turn light-shine to the door.

Black eyes turn, tossed out of clay,
see a wall's clinging chatter,
rhythm floating like paint on ghost-hands.
Museum grid-locked in talk.

Turning tossed memory, superimposed
onto the ceiling—the words come falling—
splashed glass.

ANEURISM

Before the pen interrupts
the page, it is healthy
and ink trickling transfusion
becomes the first line, the first word—breath.
Images torture, paper shivers, cracks.
Hand cannot pull back, keeps applying pressure.
Ink steeps each pore until veins flow
like trees rooting flesh.

White skin never blank again, unable to gleam
between blue-needled strokes.

Words only weak
vessels, dilated stains on a once beautiful body.
Sheet's original expanse never resuscitates,
bleeds out, drowns between its flooded walls.

MEDICATED

Cold room   rumbles   scratches
rakes up the scent   she spends an hour waiting
the water carries through—swinging calm
as a ball gown   graceful
hum rises with the cup   a swish   full of pills
and she swallows   swallows
pills fall   a new cup
her stomach a well an echo's borne into
down cold, up warm   water
swells and rises

Vocalises

ALL NIGHT

Hear the two-tone wink of sleep:
light darkness, dark lightness.
Slipping is not easy.

A ringing echoes
in cavernous tunnels
throughout the body, an acoustic tremble.

Ear jumps, cheeks blow up
near triangle pores and ingrown eyes.
Watering a memory to stay root,

but it's buried deep in the wink.
Violets float across sky,
slake boundary of yesterday.

Duplicate song bridges into blue,
wide, expanding blue.
Stillness leads gravity, drug-heavy.

Memory feels of odd time and leaves,
and nerves ready to crumble
into themselves, unvein the canals.

Gather all the air into green, grow color like moss.
It sticks, but won't stay—flings
all those who come wanting—

clangs into the stop, morning.

SILENCE

in a photograph
seems momentary,
as if a flash
holds in the next breath.
With patience potted,
a reflective pool grows,
the inks dry.
Memory only slackens
to pick up rhythm again,
and one more second
is allowed to pass.

Vocalises

ESCAPE ROUTE

Orange coat of disappointment,
you tangle my shoes into immeasurable spaces
where I can't get myself to breathe—water.

You speak in slow-rolling tongue
about tap-tripping and dancing on cotton.

Everyone listens.

Big heads float around whispering
move on to the summit, move on to the star-caves
that tackle Red Giants, swallow them whole
as ice cubes and heat to saliva—enzymatic torture-eating
at the mandarin center of it all.

Books on Pavlov peel and eat the final tendon
of self (o v e r p r e s s u r e).

Everyone reads.

With weight upon the toe of distraction
I drag the fire on, begging for unconscious hours
to dilate at every traffic light, this despite the apple
glowing in my teeth.

Can't cross all the water's humility—shrinking
under sewaged minutes. There is no taking in, no shrouding
fragile egos in lipstick stains and mango bruises
from carrying beaten poems
through the city—heaviness destroying memory
to survive all the hand tricks, the getting lost
in phone books.

Everyone follows.

And I confess! Lying in smoke-kegged eyes,
idle in the dust and sea-salty heels of evolution,
my hands do all the talking.

FEVER

Fever is fascinating,
an internal warrior
against whatever twists
the body into Rubik's Cube uncertainty.
Double-edged, positive/negative
energy stirs up the brain, confuses
night with sweat and day with T.V.
Its heat is the venom and the anti-venom,
breaks you down so you have no choice
but to fall easily into nothingness
as it releases its strength
into the blood stream like steam.

It suffers you. If you are delirious
everything finally makes sense, the closed
heavy curtains protecting eyes
as if they were the last known reservoirs.
No place else seems safe.
Only this dark warm cave,
built upon coals in the common bed,
can carry you into the next weakness.

EMBRYO

Everyone sees the splinters
wedged into your scalp. But,
"It's just your hair," they say,
as dead and empty as the last suck
from your cigarette.

The clothes you wear
say something about you.
No, not that they cover up and cook
what's inside, like dressing
packed hard into the ass of a turkey.

We see the picture, the chair, the lamp,
and the room, not the pallor boom of light
that makes us see; infinite waves licking themselves
out of existence, drowning.

And, words on a page are clear
but what about how they chase each other: racing,
showing off, cart-wheeling inside margins?

Everyone sees grit and scum flake and fall,
pounding shower tiles until the drain invites them in,
but not the sewer, which stays dark and drunk
from its own stench.

You consume music and sing it aloud
after its digestion, but no one knows
it's been fetched from your sewer,
rubbed clean of its truthful resonance,
your version of polished rocks.
Everyone sees that our own eyes whisper, a flicker,
an initiation. Handle one scene, sneak preview
the next obscenity.

Vocalises

But we ignore the transparent shield we swaddle in,
everyone's own box of cheap cellophane.
Our own eyeballs nesting, as warm
and connected as an embryo to its placenta.

VEINS

Fat ones, violet and sweet.
You like to grow them in the blue plows
of your skin, wrist punched by that knife
made from splinted wood, pine instead of oak.

But you don't want them to bleed
again while you eat them, your veins restocked,
bottles of blood instead of wine
so every time you squeeze
the juice out you taste it in your new strength
like aged Merlot.
And the dizziness is what you asked for, what you cut for.

Every day you prick more fruit,
carry it around
filling the palm of your mind
(stained oak barrel).

A new season vines down the soft of your stomach
before you begin the tearing
open (the patience it takes)—
then the full bodied smell of red summer,
of time fermenting in sealed bodies.

The excess rushes over like a shining tidal wave
where you wake up in the pit with smashed grapes
sliming under the nail of a stiffening wound.

You smell your addiction to the knife,
to pine, and to the humidity of the cellar
where you sleep, cloaked and corked
with scars, smiling and blinking on your forearms, thighs
and on your pretty face.

Vocalises

Your eyes sweat tears
slow as a cold
bowl of grapes melting out moisture—
ceremonial rain before the next stomping
of the crop.

WOMAN WRITES A LETTER

I was artless,
weaving my eyes through the windowed room
like rolling barrels
to beat the sight out of me.
Seven hundred times I have said it,
and seven hundred times
I have given away the clock.

Photographed shadow, how did you survive
the alleys and dumpsters
I sloughed you into? I am a crime.
I would pirate my lungs in exchange for a day as the moon,
I would do more. I would tiptoe
in and out
of my body,
over and over,
making every limb heavy
as Sisyphus' boulder. I would suffer if I could.
I would cry and rub the salt onto my hands,
dry as chalk, if I could.

But, night is never dark enough, my head
down in the dirt.

I would give up the gown I wear
and carry my naked skin
like a necklace on my chest.
I would do most anything to speak:
forget to ask for water.

WITH WORDS

Oceans transpose—hold the earth in their lap.

A watery shawl, worn from the racing, sprays

like silence to cool the memory—there and forgotten. Sounds

muffle where space is unyarning (sedimentary, learning

to breathe). Rivers wash away

the washing of thoughts.

TOUCHABLE

All the pressure, like a jet screaming
into its altitude. And toes disappear, tingle,
forget the earth and become boneless. Earth
with no rocks, an appendage of gravity, an after effect.
Forward motion eliminates the journey. No foot, no stretch.
Just a falling path, sliding destination. The ground
is missing, cannot mine for its memory. The sore ore
is also unattended and smells suspicious as oxygen.
Need an apple to clean the teeth
of all the accumulated fragments of moon
the sun has crackled like splinted bone, sprayed dry as dust.
And it's something, something touchable.

ACKNOWLEDGMENTS

Special thanks to Robert Booras and Zohra Saed for working so hard to publish poetry with Upset Press. You read each poem with an editor's eye, but your friendship and your faith in each one, as well as in me, has been uplifting in the world where most of my efforts to share these poems come back to me in the form of an apology. Thank you to my fellow poets who are always there to inspire, encourage, and tell painful truths, especially Denise Galang, Sean O'hanlon, Rachel Rear, Nicholas Powers, Sara Hurley, and Karen Pittelman—you are so much a part of what has created the pages in this book. Thank you to my husband, Nik, for allowing me the time and space to concentrate on writing and editing these poems. They would otherwise not exist. Thanks to all the unnamed, but not forgotten, inspirations and/or subjects of the poems themselves—most of them are people, some are not. Thank you to every reader who picks up a book of poetry and gives it a chance to be read.